P9-AFD-075

JOE BIDEN

JOE BIDEN

From Scranton to the White House

HEATHER E. SCHWARTZ

LERNER PUBLICATIONS ◆ MINNEAPOLIS

Lerner Publications Company
An imprint of Lerner Publishing Group, Inc.
241 First Avenue North
Minneapolis, MN 55401 USA

For reading levels and more information, look up this title at www.lernerbooks.com.

Image credits: David Lienemann/The White House, p. 2; AP Photo/Andrew Harnik, pp. 6, 12; David I Sanchez/Shutterstock.com, p. 9; Donlelel/Wikimedia Commons, p. 11; Bettmann/Getty Images, p. 15; AP Photo/Uncredited, p. 17; AP Photo/Gerald Herbert, p. 18; mark reinstein/Shutterstock.com, p. 20; AP Photo/Lana Harris, pp. 21, 22; AP Photo/Wilfredo Lee, p. 23; AP Photo/Adele Starr, p. 25; AP Photo/Ron Edmonds, p. 27; Rob Crandall/Shutterstock.com, p. 28; AP Photo/Barry Thumma, p. 29; AP Photo/Abaca Press, p. 31; AP Photo/J. Scott Applewhite, p. 33; AP Photo/Pat Crowe II, p. 34; AP Photo/Susan Walsh, p. 35; Kim Kelley-Wagner/Shutterstock.com, p. 37; AP Photo/Matthew Hinton, p. 39; AP Photo/Carolyn Kaster, p. 40. Cover: AP Photo/Carolyn Kaster.

Main body text set in Rotis Serif Std 55 Regular. Typeface provided by Adobe Systems.

Editor: Rebecca Higgins **Designer:** Mary Ross **Photo Editor:** Brianna Kaiser
Lerner team: Sue Marquis

Library of Congress Cataloging-in-Publication Data

Names: Schwartz, Heather E., author.
Title: Joe Biden : from Scranton to the White House / Heather E. Schwartz.
Description: Minneapolis, MN : Lerner Publications, 2021. | Series: Gateway biographies | Includes bibliographical references and index. | Audience: Ages 9–14 | Audience: Grades 4–6 | Summary: "Former Vice President Joe Biden played an essential role in the Obama administration. Follow his career from Delaware's longest-serving senator to his race back to the White House"—Provided by publisher.
Identifiers: LCCN 2020047486 (print) | LCCN 2020047487 (ebook) | ISBN 9781728420592 (library binding) | ISBN 9781728420615 (ebook)
Subjects: LCSH: Biden, Joseph R., Jr.—Juvenile literature. | Vice-presidents—United States—Biography—Juvenile literature. | Presidential candidates—United States—Biography—Juvenile literature.
Classification: LCC E840.8.B54 S45 2021 (print) | LCC E840.8.B54 (ebook) | DDC 973.932092 [B]—dc23

LC record available at https://lccn.loc.gov/2020047486
LC ebook record available at https://lccn.loc.gov/2020047487

Manufactured in the United States of America
1-49152-49300-11/9/2020

Table of Contents

Joe Biden had waited his whole career for this moment. On August 20, 2020, he stood in the Chase Center in Wilmington, Delaware, without a crowd before him. But he didn't need one. Biden accepted the nomination to be the Democratic Party candidate in the upcoming election for president of the United States.

While the COVID-19 pandemic made large gatherings unsafe, that didn't stop supporters from turning out for Biden. The Democratic National Convention moved online and became a virtual hit. About twenty-five million people watched Biden speak on-screen, while some dedicated supporters showed up in the parking lot outside the Chase Center.

Biden addressed the pandemic and promised to be a better leader than President Donald Trump was. He also talked about leading the country forward on other issues, such as the economic crisis, climate change, and the need for racial justice.

"Here and now I give you my word, if you entrust me with the presidency, I will draw on the best of us, not the worst," Biden said. "I will be an ally of the light, not the darkness. And make no mistake, united we can and will overcome this season of darkness in America. We'll choose hope over fear, facts over fiction, fairness over privilege."

Biden promised to work hard for all Americans, even those who voted against him. Many believed it was the best speech of his career. With decades of experience in politics behind him, Biden was ready to run for the highest office of all. And the win was within reach.

Struggling Student

Joseph Robinette Biden Jr. was born on November 20, 1942, in Scranton, Pennsylvania. He was the first of four children. His father, Joseph Biden Sr., was a used car salesman who also cleaned furnaces. Joe's mother, Catherine Eugenia "Jean" Finnegan, was a strong force of guidance and love for Joe and his siblings. When Joe was ten, he and his family moved to Delaware.

Growing up, Joe was bullied by other kids. They called him names and made fun of him for stuttering. His parents taught him to be tough and to stand up for himself, even if it meant physically fighting bullies in the neighborhood.

Joe also worked on his speech. He memorized poetry

and recited it in front of the mirror. He still stuttered, but he had more control over his words.

"I never had professional therapy, but a couple of nuns taught me to put a cadence to my speaking, and that's why I spent so much time reading poetry—Emerson and Yeats," he said. "But even in my small, boys' prep school, I got nailed in Latin class with the nickname Joe Impedimenta. You get so desperate, you're so embarrassed."

Joe loves his hometown, Scranton.

Joe dreamed of attending Archmere Academy, a private school across the street from his house. At the age of fourteen, he was accepted. He washed windows and weeded gardens at the school to offset the tuition. He was small and skinny, but he became a star football player. He was also elected class president during his junior and senior years. The only election he lost was for captain of the football team. One of his proudest moments during high school was a more personal win. As a sophomore, he fulfilled a school requirement by speaking in front of his class.

After graduating in 1961, Biden went on to the University of Delaware. During his first two years of college, he focused more on football and parties than his schoolwork. But in his junior year, he became interested in politics. He settled into studying history and political science.

While on spring break in the Bahamas, Biden met Neilia Hunter. She studied English and teaching at Syracuse University. The two immediately hit it off. After Biden graduated from the University of Delaware in 1965, he attended Syracuse University Law School so he could be close to Neilia. While he studied law, she pursued her master's degree in English and taught at a public school. The couple married in 1966.

Biden already had dreams of going into politics and even becoming president of the United States. But he wasn't a stellar student in law school. During his first year, he was accused of plagiarism. He had failed to

Biden has maintained his connection to Syracuse University throughout his political career.

properly cite a reference to a law review article. He claimed it was a mistake, but he still had to take the course over, and a letter about the incident was added to his file.

"To me, law school was just like college; all I had to do was get through to graduation, and I could get moving on real life," Biden said. "The work didn't seem so hard, just boring, and I was a dangerous combination of arrogant and sloppy. I'm not sure I even bought all the books I was supposed to have first semester. And I was

Giving Back

Biden worked hard on his speaking skills, and he also helped others do the same. One person he helped was Brayden Harrington, a thirteen-year-old boy he met on the 2020 campaign trail.

When Biden heard Brayden's stutter, he invited him backstage to talk. Biden explained how he worked on his stutter and how he marked his speeches to make them easier to deliver.

Brayden later used the technique when he delivered a speech supporting Biden at the Democratic National Convention. He said he felt more confident since talking with Biden and urged people to vote for him.

Biden embraces Brayden in 2020.

a less-than-frequent visitor to class. . . . The truth was, I hadn't been to class enough to know how to do citations in a legal brief."

Biden buckled down in order to pass his classes. His hard work paid off as he earned higher grades. He learned to love public speaking and grew interested in a career as a trial lawyer.

Starting Out

In 1968 Biden graduated from law school near the bottom of his class. Despite his grades, people knew he was ambitious and could work hard. His law school file was filled with recommendations from professors, and he landed a job with a law firm in Delaware.

After a short time there, Biden realized it wasn't the right place for him. The firm represented big corporations. He wanted to represent individuals who needed help. In 1969 he began to work as a public defender. That year, he and Neilia had their first child, Joseph Robinette Biden III, whom they called Beau.

As an attorney and father, Biden was much more driven than he had been as a student. He and Neilia invested in real estate. Biden also took on additional work managing a private swimming pool so the family could live on country club grounds for free. In 1970 the family grew with the birth of Robert Hunter Biden, known as Hunter.

Biden was busy, but he still had an interest in politics. He spent Wednesday evenings at Democratic Forum meetings, and soon he ran for the New Castle County Council. The area was mostly Republican, but with Neilia's support, he decided to do it. His sister, Val, ran his campaign, and Biden spent a lot of time going door-to-door, talking to voters about how he could help them. When he won the election in November, he took his first political position as a member of the county council. His work aligned with his values.

"My first year on the county council, I became known as the guy who took on the builders and the big corporations," he said. "I was all for businesses creating jobs and wealth, but I thought the companies that would profit owed a fair accounting of the real costs."

Biden and Neilia grew even busier when their third child, Naomi Christina Biden, was born in 1971. That year Biden worked on building his own law firm and strengthening the Democratic Party in his state. He joined with other Democratic leaders to form the Democratic Renewal Commission to modernize the party and its campaign techniques so it would be more relevant to voters. They began looking for a strong candidate who could run for one of Delaware's US Senate seats the following year. Everyone they asked turned them down. Biden was shocked when two elders of the Delaware Democratic Party eventually asked him. "My initial reaction was: I don't think I'm old enough," he said. "I had to do the math."

Biden celebrates his thirtieth birthday with Neilia and their sons.

According to the US Constitution, senators must be at least thirty years old. Biden would turn thirty just in time to be sworn in—if he was elected. It was a long shot to run against the Republican incumbent, J. Caleb Boggs, who had been in office since 1946. But Biden's whole family was behind him and willing to help. Once again, Val ran his campaign. His brother Frank recruited young volunteers, and his brother Jimmy took on fundraising. His mother and Neilia organized hundreds of events throughout the state where Biden could meet and talk personally with voters. He also educated himself by meeting with professors, lawyers, and judges to learn more about the issues. Biden knew he had to be sharp when it came to understanding the tax code, the Vietnam War (1954–1975), the environment, crime, and other important issues.

By the time he publicly announced his intention to run, Biden was ready not just for the race, but for the job ahead. In November 1972, he was elected to the US Senate. He would be the country's fifth-youngest senator in history.

Tragic Loss, New Beginnings

Winning the Senate seat was a major victory for Biden and his family. Even before he took office, the media started predicting he was headed for the White House. Biden felt the pieces of his life had fallen into place. He had a loving wife, three beautiful children, and a successful start to a political career.

Christmas was only a week away when Biden left Delaware with Val to do some work in Washington, DC. Neilia stayed home to finish shopping with the children. Biden and Val were together in an office when a call came in from Jimmy. Neilia and the children had been in a car accident. Biden had to go home right away.

It was worse than anyone wanted to tell Biden on the phone. His wife and daughter had died in the crash.

Beau had several broken bones. Hunter had head injuries. Angry and upset, Biden focused on caring for his sons.

"I could not speak, only felt this hollow core grow in my chest, like I was going to be sucked inside a black hole," Biden said. "Most of all I was numb, but there were moments when the pain cut through like a shard of broken glass."

Biden's Senate seat no longer felt important. He considered giving it up. But as the weeks passed, he realized Neilia wouldn't want him to walk away from the victory they'd fought for together. He decided to try the job for six months. But he refused to leave his boys to go to Washington, DC, to be sworn in. Instead, on January 5, 1973, he was sworn into office in the Wilmington hospital where Beau and Hunter were staying.

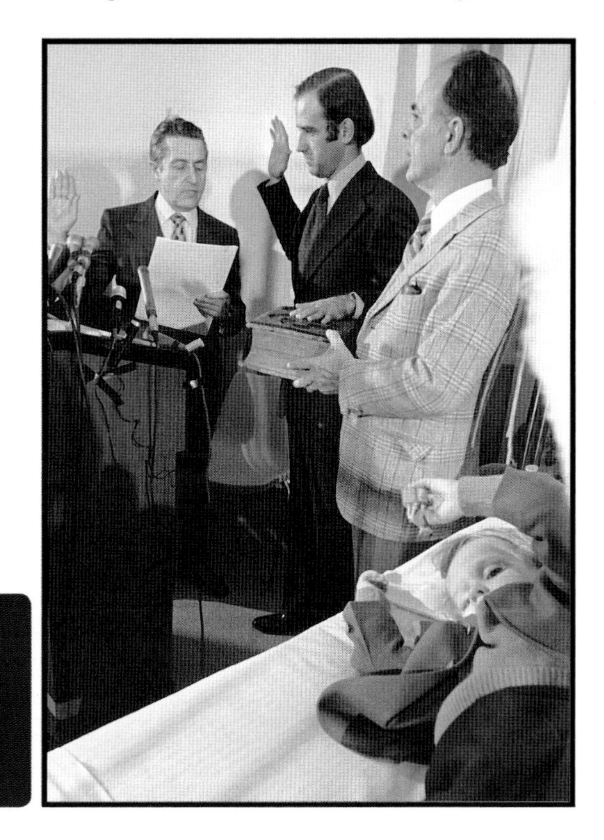

Biden takes the oath of office in the hospital where his sons were recovering.

Biden felt he had to keep going with his political career. He had to be a professional. But his joy and passion for the job were gone. When the boys were released from the hospital, Val and her husband moved in with the family to help care for them. Each day, Biden took an Amtrak train to his job in Washington, DC. The round trip took three hours, but he gained time with his boys in the morning before dropping them off at school, and he was home in time to tuck them in at night. Over time, he earned a nickname among his colleagues: Amtrak Joe. All he really cared about was getting

Biden still enjoys traveling via Amtrak trains.

home to his sons and proving he would always be there for them.

The boys healed, and Biden began to see how lucky he was to work with so many people in the Senate who cared about him. They invited him to dinners and insisted he show up. His friend Fritz Hollings made a point of making him feel wanted, and Hollings's wife, Peatsy, always confirmed the time and place beforehand. Biden grew closer to his friend Stuart Symington, who had also recently lost his wife. Biden started to feel more comfortable in his new life and more interested in the issues he faced as a US senator. He was beginning to rebuild his life. "As time passed and the day of the accident receded, I found I was happy to be there and fully engaged," he said. "The issues in my first term were not small."

Two years after the accident, Biden's life began to change again. After reluctantly agreeing to a blind date set up by his brother Frank, he fell in love with Jill Jacobs, an English teacher. His boys fell in love with her too. One morning, seven-year-old Beau told him they'd decided he should marry Jill.

Biden agreed and proposed. Jill loved him and the boys. But she'd been married and divorced before, and she took her time making the decision. Biden proposed four more times before she said yes. In 1977 Biden and Jill were married with Beau and Hunter standing by them at the altar. They became a blended family that included the memories of Neilia and Naomi.

Biden and Jill smile together in 1987.

In 1978 Biden won reelection to the Senate. In 1981 he and Jill had a baby girl, Ashley Blazer Biden. Despite his tragic losses, Biden was picking up the pieces and building a new life.

A Bid for Biden

As Biden continued his career in the Senate, he distinguished himself as a leader by expanding his knowledge and taking strong stances on important issues. Some of his opinions were controversial. While he supported civil rights, he voted against forcing the Department of Education to bus students in order to desegregate schools. He also supported tough crime laws such as the Comprehensive Crime Control Act and the Anti-Drug Abuse Act of 1986. Both laws expanded penalties for drug crimes.

In 1987 Biden became chair of the Senate Judiciary Committee, a group of twenty-two senators that oversees the Department of Justice. That year, he decided to make a run for the highest office in the country. On June 9 in Wilmington, he launched a campaign to become president of the United States. If elected, he

Biden (*second from right*) talks with other members of the Senate Judiciary Committee in 1986.

Biden (*at the podium, on right*) launches his campaign for president alongside his family and supporters.

would become the country's third-youngest president at forty-four years of age. "He was considered by quite a few people as a bright new hope, different from other Democrats," said Laurence I. Barrett, a former *Time* magazine political correspondent.

But in September 1987, Biden made a grave error at the Iowa State Fair. He plagiarized part of a speech given by Neil Kinnock, a politician running for office in the United Kingdom. The media ran with the story and soon discovered another speech Biden had

Biden on Busing

As a first-term US senator, Biden had to fully understand the issues the country was facing. One of those issues involved busing students. In the 1970s, busing was used to integrate schools that were segregated by race.

When the Senate decided whether the US Department of Education should mandate busing, Biden opposed the idea. Kamala Harris, who became a senator in 2017, challenged Biden on his position when the two ran for the 2020 presidential nomination. She was bused to school as a little girl and believed Biden should have supported busing.

Biden explained that he did support integrating schools. But he opposed busing in the 1970s because he didn't believe the federal government should force schools to do it. After Biden became the Democratic Party nominee for president, he chose Harris as his running mate.

Biden (*left*) and Harris (*right*) discuss busing in a 2019 debate.

plagiarized in February. A video surfaced in which he spoke angrily to a voter and exaggerated his academic record. Reporters also uncovered Biden's plagiarism in law school.

Biden denied purposely plagiarizing or misstating the facts, but he was unable to recover from the negative press. On September 24, 1987, he withdrew from the race. It was a disheartening time in his career. But by February 1988, he had plans to get out and face the public again. He accepted invitations to speak at the University of Rochester, the Rochester Institute of Technology in New York, and Yale University in Connecticut. He prepared himself to answer difficult questions and prove that he was staying on the path of public service.

Despite his tough-minded resolve, Biden couldn't shake off the physical problems he'd started experiencing. He carried pain relievers with him everywhere for continuous headaches. He developed pains in his neck and numbness on his right side. A doctor gave him a neck brace and special exercises to do. Biden carried on with his travel plans.

On February 9, Biden felt good after an especially warm reception at the University of Rochester. He went to his hotel room planning to order some food. The next thing he knew, he was waking up on the floor, disoriented and in terrible pain. By the time he got to the hospital, doctors didn't expect him to live. He had a brain aneurysm that was bleeding and required surgery.

Biden talks to the press after being hospitalized for a blood clot with Hunter at his side.

Even if he survived, his brain might be damaged. Doctors warned he could lose his speech.

Biden survived the surgery without damage to his brain. But recovery would be a long and difficult road. He developed a blood clot in his lung that required another hospital stay and operation. The doctors caught another aneurysm before it could burst. Biden had to undergo surgery to repair it.

Months passed before Biden was able to return to his normal life. During his recovery, Biden learned Michael

Dukakis had won the Democratic Party nomination for president. Dukakis would run against George H. W. Bush in the November election. Biden's first public appearance was at an event in Delaware in late August.

"All I wanted to do was assure them that I was back to serve in the Senate to the best of my abilities," he said. "I had had a lot of time to think about my past and my future, and I wanted to be in the Senate for years to come. For good or ill, I was a public man. I was a lucky man, to be sure."

Continuing His Senate Career

After being knocked down in his bid for president and again by his health problems, Biden was finally back to business in the Senate. And he had a lot of work to do.

Senate Terms

The term of office for a US senator is six years. After his election in 1972, Biden was reelected to the Senate six times, in 1978, 1984, 1990, 1996, 2002, and 2008. He also served in other ways. He chaired the Judiciary Committee from 1987 to 1995. He was a member of the Senate's Foreign Relations Committee and served as chair from 2001 to 2003 and from 2007 to 2009.

Biden is welcomed back to the Senate in 1988.

In 1991 Biden oversaw the Supreme Court confirmation hearings for Clarence Thomas. Just before the Senate approved Thomas's nomination, he was accused of sexual harassment by former colleague Anita Hill. Biden asked the White House to authorize the FBI to investigate Thomas. The Senate vote was postponed, but the hearings continued.

At the hearings, Biden did little to stop Republican committee members from verbally attacking Hill. He also failed to call three women to testify with stories

Hill testifies during Clarence Thomas's confirmation hearings.

that might have supported Hill's allegations. Biden was criticized for his choices, but he felt defending Hill more strongly would have required breaking the rules of the Senate. When it came time to vote, he voted against Thomas, but in the end Thomas was confirmed. Biden later apologized for his role in hearings that didn't treat Hill fairly.

His failure to protect Hill hurt Biden's standing with women. So when he supported the Violence Against Women Act, some said he was trying to make up for the past and win over women voters. But Biden cared deeply about helping women who'd been victims of violence. He visited women's shelters and other organizations. He worked with his staff to release a report that explained how important the bill was.

"The twenty-page timeline of narratives culled from a week's worth of business at police stations, battered women's shelters, and rape crisis centers was horrifying," he said. "If we had included all we knew in the timeline, it would have run two thousand pages."

The Violence Against Women Act was part of another crime bill Biden supported that was more controversial: the Violent Crime Control and Law Enforcement Act.

Biden discusses the Violence Against Women Act in 1993.

When it passed in 1994, it created funding for more prisons and police officers and demanded tougher prison sentences. The Violence Against Women Act also gave government funding to rape crisis centers, women's shelters, legal assistance programs, and other programs to help women who'd been victims of violence.

As Biden continued his Senate career, he made his mark in foreign relations as well as criminal justice. He spoke out in support of US action to protect Kosovo during the late 1990s. He believed America's military should strike against Serbian forces that were attacking Kosovars. In 2002 he voted in support of President George W. Bush's decision to start the Iraq War (2003–2011), meant to capture the country's alleged stash of weapons of mass destruction. In 2007, after the US had determined Iraq was not stockpiling weapons, Biden opposed Bush's decision to send in more troops.

In 2007 Biden published his autobiography, *Promises to Keep: On Life and Politics*. In the book, he revealed he was considering running for president again in the 2008 election. His vision for the country included bringing people together. He was optimistic about what he could achieve as America's leader.

"I see a future in which Americans remember that when we value what we hold in common above all else, there is nothing we cannot achieve," he said. "The vision of that future is what keeps me going because it is absolutely within our reach."

Biden and Obama wave at the crowd at the 2008 Democratic National Convention.

Vice President Joe Biden

Biden may have been looking for a path to the presidency in 2007. But he found a different way to the White House. In January 2008 he dropped out of the presidential race, realizing he couldn't win the Democratic Party nomination. Seven months later, Democratic presidential nominee Barack Obama chose Biden as his running mate.

Obama felt Biden's knowledge of foreign relations would complement his own areas of expertise. Biden, who grew up in Scranton, Pennsylvania, also created a connection with working-class voters. Biden had seen his father fall on hard times, take a blue-collar position cleaning boilers, and work hard to make ends meet.

When Obama announced his choice, he talked about all that Biden had overcome in his life, from the tragedy that took Neilia and Naomi to his health challenges. "Joe Biden's many triumphs have come only after great trial," Obama said. "He raised his family with a strong commitment to work and to family, to the Catholic faith, and to the belief that in America you can make it if you try. Those are the core values that Joe Biden has carried with him to this day."

Obama and Biden ran against Republican presidential candidate John McCain, a senator from Arizona, and his running mate, Sarah Palin, the governor of Alaska. On November 4, 2008, Obama was elected the country's first Black president with 364 electoral votes. The win made Biden vice president.

Though Biden also won reelection to the Senate that year, he resigned before taking his new office in January 2009. Working with President Obama, Biden focused on issues including foreign relations, raising living standards for middle-class Americans, and reducing gun violence and violence against women. After a financial crisis in 2008, Biden was heavily involved in passing the Recovery Act in February. He oversaw $800 billion to turn around the economy by creating and saving jobs.

Biden (*second from left*) and other politicians watch as Obama signs the Affordable Care Act into law.

Biden also worked with President Obama to pass the Affordable Care Act. The law offered health insurance to twenty million uninsured Americans. It also forbade insurance companies from turning people away for having preexisting health problems.

In 2012 Obama and Biden ran for office again, this time against Republican Mitt Romney and his running mate, Representative Paul Ryan. The Democratic ticket won 332 electoral votes, and Obama and Biden were set to serve in the White House for another four years.

Losing a Son

In 2015 Biden endured another personal tragedy. His oldest son, Beau, who had followed him into politics, died of brain cancer at the age of forty-six. Biden said that when Beau knew he was dying, he'd encouraged his father to stick with his political career.

"It didn't mean I had to run for president, but he was worried I would walk away from what I've worked on my whole life," Biden said. "He is a part of me, and so is my surviving son, Hunter, and Ashley."

Beau celebrates being elected Delaware's attorney general with Jill and Biden.

Biden still had work to do—and new crises to manage. After a tragic shooting incident at Sandy Hook Elementary School in Newtown, Connecticut, Biden led efforts to end gun violence, including creating more extensive background checks for people who wanted to buy guns. President Obama also put him in charge of government efforts to prevent, diagnose, and treat cancer, aiming to make ten years' worth of improvements in just five years.

Just before their term ended in January 2017, Obama surprised his vice president. Biden thought he was going to a gathering to toast the senior White House staff. But Obama awarded him with the Presidential Medal of Freedom. It was the nation's highest civilian honor.

Biden tears up as Obama presents him with the Presidential Medal of Freedom.

Obama spoke of Biden's honesty, optimism, and vision, all of which made him a great vice president. "I had no inkling," Biden said, before thanking his wife, his children, and others who'd supported him along the way.

Biden for President

After eight years in Washington, DC, as vice president and second lady, Biden and Jill returned to their Delaware home. Together, they continued to serve the public. In February 2017, they established the Biden Foundation to work on issues they are passionate about, including making college affordable, creating jobs for military spouses, and ending violence against women.

Second Lady Dr. Jill Biden

As second lady of the United States, Dr. Jill Biden both supported her husband and worked to support the causes she cared about. She worked full-time as an English professor at a North Virginia community college. She believed strongly in community colleges and worked to promote them. A military mom to Beau, she worked closely with Michelle Obama on the Joining Forces initiative to support military families. She also started the Biden Breast Health Initiative to support early breast cancer detection after three of her friends were diagnosed with the disease.

In Charlottesville, Virginia, white supremacists meet counterprotesters that oppose their hate.

Biden was also ready to lead two academic centers. The Penn Biden Center for Diplomacy and Global Engagement focused on diplomacy, foreign policy, and national security. The Biden Institute at the University of Delaware focused on domestic policy.

In June 2017, Biden and Jill founded the Biden Cancer Initiative. It continued the work they had begun with the Biden Breast Health Initiative.

A couple of months later, in August 2017, Biden watched along with the rest of the US as white supremacists marched in Charlottesville, Virginia, an event that led to the death of a counterprotester. White supremacists spread hate about anyone who is not white.

Name-Calling in the News

Trump called Biden Sleepy Joe in an attempt to undermine him in the presidential race. Biden told the media he wanted to avoid sinking to the president's level by resorting to name-calling. "On every single issue and on every demeaning thing he says about other people, I have no problem responding directly," Biden said in 2019. "What I'm not going to do is get into what he wants me to do."

Like many Americans, he was horrified when President Donald Trump spoke out to defend the white supremacists instead of condemning them. "In that moment I knew that the threat to this nation was unlike any I'd seen in my lifetime," Biden said.

He'd been considering another run for president for months. Now he felt the decision was clear. He had to run against Trump. In April 2019, he made his announcement.

"If we give Donald Trump eight years in the White House, he will forever and fundamentally alter the character of this nation, who we are, and I cannot stand by and watch that happen," Biden said. "The core values of this nation, our standing in the world, our very democracy, everything that has made America America is at stake."

As Biden's campaign took off, the media reported that Trump was pressuring the president of Ukraine to investigate the Biden family's connections there. Trump claimed Biden was using his power to benefit Hunter's work in Ukraine. Trump threatened to illegally withhold military aid to Ukraine unless the investigation took place. But many believed Trump's true aim was to damage Biden's credibility and help his own chances in the 2020 election.

No evidence was found against the Bidens. However, the US House of Representatives brought impeachment charges against Trump for his call to Ukraine. He was charged with abusing his power and obstructing Congress, and he was impeached in December. His impeachment trial lasted nearly three weeks. In the end, the Senate acquitted him in February 2020.

Biden speaks at a campaign event in 2019.

Harris accepts the vice-presidential nomination and talks of her and Biden's plan for the country.

By the end of June 2020, polls showed Biden pulling ahead of Trump in several swing states that could determine the election. On August 11, Biden announced he'd chosen his running mate: Senator Kamala Harris. She made history as the first Black woman and first Asian woman to be on a presidential ticket.

A week later, delegates appeared on-screen at the virtual Democratic National Convention, announcing their votes for Biden and expressing their support. His home state of Delaware sealed the deal, and he was officially named the Democratic Party presidential nominee.

Supporters clapped and cheered as the song "Celebration" by Kool & the Gang played in the background. When the camera turned to Biden, streamers flew behind him while family members danced and smiled. "Thank you very, very much from the bottom of my heart," he said. "It means the world to me and my family."

Biden was poised to face the challenges ahead. He was ready to win the election and become the forty-sixth president of the United States.

On November 7, 2020, the media declared the election's winner. It took several days to count the ballots, many of which had been mailed in due to COVID-19. Biden was pronounced the president-elect. Harris was pronounced vice president elect. Their supporters danced and cheered in the streets in celebration.

Trump rejected the results and filed lawsuits against them, but they were thrown out for lack of evidence. People close to him suggested that he concede.

Meanwhile, Biden got to work. He wouldn't be inaugurated until January 20, 2021, but he wanted to be ready on day one. He named a coronavirus task force to take control of the pandemic. He also worked on policies addressing the economy, racial justice, and climate. He was prepared to lead and be a president for all Americans.

IMPORTANT DATES

1942	Joseph Robinette Biden Jr. is born on November 20.
1972	He is elected to the United States Senate in November.
	Neilia and Naomi are killed in a car accident that also injures Beau and Hunter in December.
1977	Biden marries his second wife, Jill Jacobs.
1987	Biden launches a campaign to run for president of the United States in June.
	He withdraws from the race in September.
1988	He suffers from brain aneurysms.
1991	Biden oversees the Supreme Court confirmation hearings for Clarence Thomas.
	He helps pass the Violence Against Women Act.
2008	Biden is elected vice president of the United States.
2012	Biden is reelected vice president of the United States.
2015	Beau dies of brain cancer.

2017 President Barack Obama awards Biden the Presidential Medal of Freedom.

2019 Biden announces he is running for president of the United States.

2020 Biden wins the Democratic nomination.

Biden is elected president of the United States.

SOURCE NOTES

8 "Joe Biden's DNC Speech," CNN, accessed October 2, 2020, https://www.cnn.com/videos/politics/2020/08/21/joe-biden-dnc-2020-speech-full-video-vpx.cnn/video/playlists/atv-2020-dnc-full-speeches/.

9 "Joe Biden Opens Up about Childhood Stuttering Problem," *People*, March 9, 2011, https://people.com/celebrity/joe-biden-opens-up-about-childhood-stuttering-problem/.

11, 13 Jackson Schroeder, "Joe Biden's Life as a College Student," University Network, accessed October 2, 2020, https://www.tun.com/blog/joe-bidens-life-as-a-college-student/.

14 Joe Biden, *Promises to Keep: On Life and Politics* (New York: Random House, 2007), 51.

14 Biden, 57.

17 Biden, 80.

19 Biden, 104.

22 Olivia B. Waxman, "Why Joe Biden's First Campaign for President Collapsed after Just 3 Months," *Time*, August 2, 2019, https://time.com/5636715/biden-1988-presidential-campaign/.

26 Biden, *Promises*, 233.

29 Biden, 259.

30 Biden, 364.

32 "Sen. Obama Introduces VP Pick Joe Biden," YouTube video, 16:51, posted by C-SPAN, August 23, 2008, https://www.youtube.com/watch?v=lqpIe1bC6tA.

34 Grace Panetta, "Joe Biden Said His Late Son Beau 'Should Be the One Running for President' in an Emotional Tribute on 'Morning Joe,'" Business Insider, January 22, 2020, https://www.businessinsider.com/joe-biden-late-son-beau-should-be-running-for-president-2020-1.

36 Kevin Liptak and Allie Malloy, "Biden Awarded Presidential Medal of Freedom," CNN, January 13, 2017, https://www.cnn.com/2017/01/12/politics/biden-awarded-presidential-medal-of-freedom/index.html.

38 John Haltiwanger, "Joe Biden Has a New Nickname for Trump after the President Called Him 'Sleepy Joe,'" Business Insider, May 10, 2019, https://www.businessinsider.com/joe-biden-has-nickname-for-trump-after-president-called-him-sleepy-joe-2019-5.

38 "Joe Biden Formally Announces 2020 Run for President," YouTube video, 9:57, posted by CNN, April 25, 2019, https://www.youtube.com/watch?v=JQsY12ARmSQ.

38 "Joe Biden Formally Announces 2020 Run for President."

41 Toluse Olorunnipa, Chelsea Janes, Felicia Sonmez, Colby Itkowitz, and John Wagner, "Joe Biden Officially Becomes the Democratic Party's Nominee on Convention's Second Night," *Washington Post*, August 18, 2020, https://www.washingtonpost.com/elections/2020/08/18/democratic-national-convention-live-updates/.

SELECTED BIBLIOGRAPHY

Biden, Joe. *Promises to Keep: On Life and Politics.* New York: Random House, 2007.

Menas, Amanda. "Who Is Dr. Jill Biden? 7 Things You Need to Know." National Education Association, April 23, 2020. https://educationvotes.nea.org/2020/04/23/who-is-dr-jill-biden-7-things-you-need-to-know/.

Newman, Meredith. "Joe Biden's Family Tree: An Introduction to Delaware's Most Famous Family." *Delaware News Journal*, August 14, 2020. https://www.delawareonline.com/story/news/politics/joe-biden/2019/04/25/joe-biden-running-2020-a-look-at-biden-family/3013958002/.

Perticone, Joe. "Flashback: Joe Biden's First Presidential Run in 1988 Cratered amid Multiple Instances of Plagiarism." Business Insider, March 12, 2019. https://www.businessinsider.com/plagiarism-scandal-joe-biden-first-presidential-run-1988-2019-3.

"Sen. Obama Introduces VP Pick Joe Biden." YouTube video, 16:51. Posted by C-SPAN, August 23, 2008. https://www.youtube.com/watch?v=lqpIe1bC6tA.

Stanton, Zack, and Jordan Muller. "55 Things You Need to Know about Joe Biden." *Politico*, March 5, 2020. https://www.politico.com/news/magazine/2020/03/05/biden-2020-president-facts-what-you-should-know-campaign-121422.

Taylor, Jessica. "In a Surprise Send-Off, Obama Awards Biden Presidential Medal of Freedom." NPR, January 12, 2017. https://www.npr.org/2017/01/12/509545778/in-surprise-send-off-president-obama-awards-biden-presidential-medal-of-freedom.

Timm, Jane C. "There's No Evidence for Trump's Biden-Ukraine Accusations. What Really Happened?" NBC News, September 25, 2019. https://www.nbcnews.com/politics/2020-election/there-s-no-evidence-trump-s-biden-ukraine-accusations-what-n1057851.

LEARN MORE

Biography: Joe Biden
https://www.biography.com/political-figure/joe-biden

Britannica: Joe Biden
https://www.britannica.com/biography/Joe-Biden

Gormley Beatrice. *Joe Biden: A Biography for Young Readers.* New York: Aladdin, 2021.

Morlock, Rachael. *Barack Obama: A Life of Leadership.* New York: Lucent, 2020.

Obama White House: Vice President Joe Biden
https://obamawhitehouse.archives.gov/vp

Schwartz, Heather E. *Kamala Harris: Madam Vice President.* Minneapolis: Lerner Publications, 2021.

INDEX